KU-737-523

THIS BOOK BELONGS TO

....

Copyright © 2016

make believe ideas ltd

The Wilderness, Berkhamsted, Hertfordshire, HP4 2AZ, UK.

All rights reserved. No part of this publication may be
reproduced, stored in a retrieval system, or transmitted
in any form or by any means, electronic, mechanical,
photocopying, recording, or otherwise, without the
prior written permission of the copyright owner.

www.makebelieveideas.com

NOAH'S ARK

-- AND OTHER BIBLE STORIES --

Illustrated by Dawn Machell

Written by Hayley Down

make
believe
ideas

CREATION

God made **everything** you can see:
the sky, the earth, and one **special tree**.
He put **Eve** and **Adam** in a place
where they would **live** in His good grace.

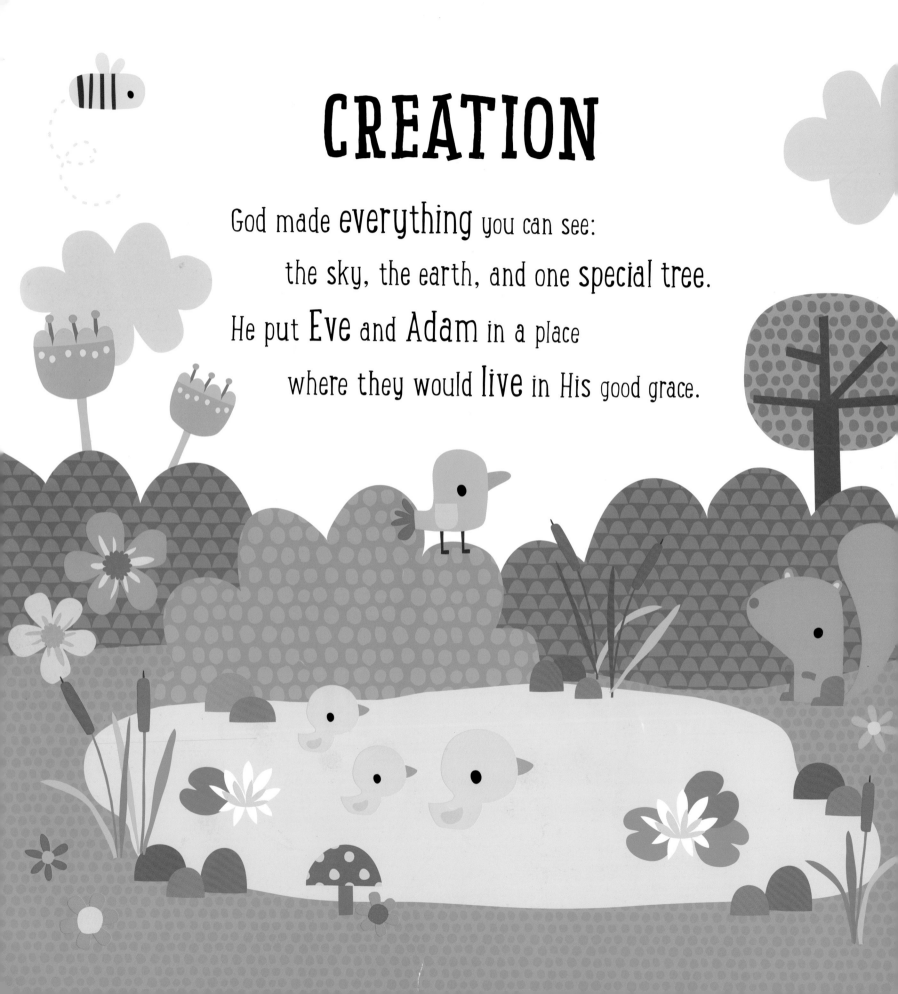

Then, a **serpent** tempted Eve
to **eat** from the forbidden **tree**.

Adam and **Eve** left Eden that day,
for they had **chosen** their **own** way.

NOAH

Noah was faithful, true, and good.

God told him, "Build an **ark** of wood."

He built the boat and – **two by two** –

brought in **animals** and his family, too.

The **rain** came down for **forty** days,

and the **flood** washed all our **sins** away.

Later, when all the land was dry,
a **rainbow** appeared in the **sky**.

JOSEPH

Old Jacob had **twelve** special sons,

but gave a **coat** to only one.

Joseph **dreamt** he would rule one day,

so his brothers sent him **far** away.

But with hard work, he did **succeed**,
and **helped** people who were in need.

The **pharaoh** dreamt **famine** would come,
but Joseph's plans saved **everyone!**

MOSES

Moses was found in the water
and taken in by the king's daughter.
But Moses left his wealth and fame
and began to work in God's name.

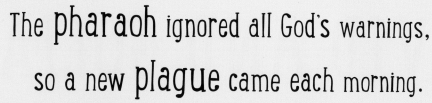

The **pharaoh** ignored all God's warnings,
so a new **plague** came each morning.

God helped Moses to **part** the **sea**
and **set** all of his **people** free.

DAVID AND GOLIATH

A war broke out in David's land,
led by Goliath, so tall and grand.
Goliath shouted to the men,
"Beat me, and we won't fight again."

With faith, young David threw a stone,
and Goliath fell down with a groan.
God helped David to win the fight –
proving faith is stronger than might.

DANIEL

Daniel was **trusted** by the king,
so he looked after **everything**.
But **jealous** men made **prayer** a crime,
then **spied** on Daniel at prayer time.

They threw him in the lions' den,
for his prayers had angered them.

But there was no need for alarm;
God kept Daniel safe from harm!

THE NATIVITY

An angel told Mary she'd give birth

to a Son who would save the earth.

Jesus was born one quiet night

under a star that shone so bright.

Some shepherds came from far to see
the Son of God – and this was He!
The shepherds quickly spread the news:
today is born the King of the Jews.

FEEDING OF THE 5,000

Five thousand people came one day
to hear what Jesus had to say.
Just as lunchtime had begun,
some had food and some had none.

One small boy had **fish** and bread –
and with just this, the **crowd** was fed!
For **Jesus** performed a **miracle**,
making **food** for **one** and all!

THE GOOD SAMARITAN

Here's a **story** that Jesus told:

A man was **robbed** of clothes and gold.

Two **men** walked **past** and heard him **yelp**,

but **neither** man **stopped** by to help.

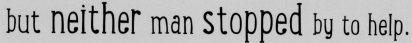

A Samaritan was passing by,
and came to **help** when he heard the cry!

Kind **things** like this show us God's love
and the **heart** of our **Father** above.

EASTER

Jesus journeyed from town to town
to spread God's message all around.
He was put to death upon a cross
but hope for us all was not lost.

He lay for **three** days in a tomb,
but then He **rose** up from the gloom!

When He died, He **saved** us from sin
and now we **praise** and worship Him.